SIMPLY
SALADS

Consultant Editor:
Valerie Ferguson

LORENZ BOOKS

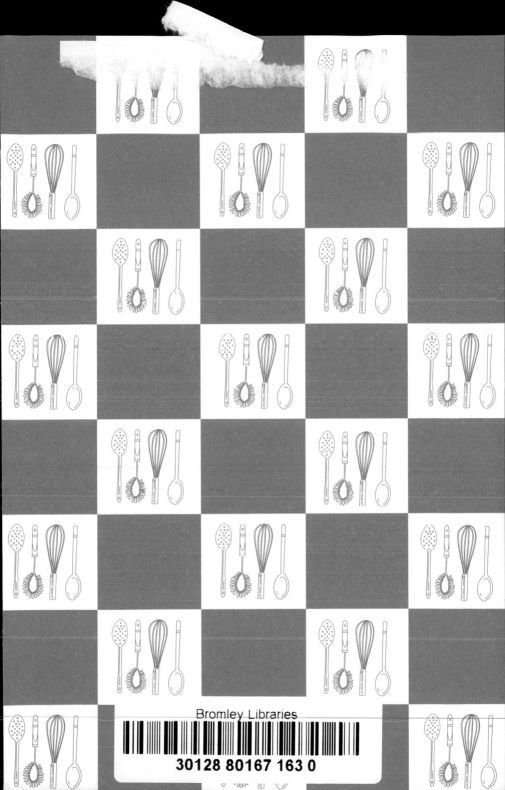

Contents

Introduction

A well-made salad is almost lyrical in its combination of fresh tastes, textures and colours expressing a particular mood or theme. This book looks at a variety of salad ideas and shows that there is more to salads than just a few lettuce leaves, cucumber and a sliced tomato.

Seasonal changes are important and provide a useful lead when you are searching for inspiration. The finest salads begin with one or two ingredients that may catch the attention. If, say, a freshly boiled crab takes your fancy, consider the rich flavours of avocado, fresh coriander (cilantro) leaves and lime; some new potatoes and young lettuce leaves will make it a dish to remember.

Salads can be cold or warm, made with meat, poultry or fish, leaves, vegetables, nuts or fruit – or any combination of these. The recipes in this book range from simple classics, such as Caesar Salad, to robust main courses, including Roast Pepper & Wild Mushroom Pasta Salad. Whatever your choice, always remember that where two or more ingredients combine, their flavours and textures should marry well together but should also still be individually identifiable. May your salads bring good health and happiness to your table!

Salad Ingredients

The choice of salad ingredients and flavourings is infinite, encompassing crisp leaves, succulent vegetables and fruit, and aromatic herbs and spices.

COS LETTUCE The cos lettuce, which originated on the Greek island of Cos, has a robust, slightly bitter flavour. Cos is the preferred salad leaf for Caesar salad.

ESCAROLE This is a robust green salad leaf that, like frisée and chicory, has a bitter flavour. It is best during the winter months and is usually served with a sweet dressing.

FRISÉE LETTUCE Also known as curly endive, frisée is a member of the chicory family. It has a clean, bitter taste that combines well with sweeter salad leaves such as young spinach.

ICEBERG LETTUCE The tightly packed iceberg lettuce has a crisp texture. It is suited to fine shredding and combines well with strong dressings and other salad leaves.

LAMB'S LETTUCE The delicate leaves of lamb's lettuce or corn salad grow year round. These are eaten whole and have a mild, sweet flavour.

LITTLE GEM (BIBB) LETTUCE This is a small, sweet, compact lettuce similar in flavour to cos. Its well-formed leaves are inclined to keep longer than those of many other lettuce varieties.

Oak leaf

Radicchio

Frisée

Chicory (Endive)

Cos

Escarole

Lamb's lettuce

Little Gem (Bibb)

Rocket (Arugula)

LOLLO ROSSO Also called red lollo, this is a mild-flavoured lettuce with a curly edge. This loose-leaved variety is appreciated for its decorative purple-red tinted leaves.

OAK LEAF LETTUCE The broad, wavy leaves of oak leaf or feuille de chêne are tinted a purple-brown. Its dark colour and mild taste combine well with the bitter leaves of escarole and frisée.

RADICCHIO This variety of chicory has purplish-red leaves with pronounced cream veins. It is bitter in flavour and best used in small quantities with other salad leaves.

ROCKET (ARUGULA) With its peppery taste of lemon, rocket is often combined with milder leaves to add flavour and zest. Rocket leaves keep well when immersed in cold water.

CHICORY Also known as Belgian endive, chicory is superbly versatile. Use the leaves in salads or as decorative canapé holders. Keep in a cool, dark place as it is sensitive to light and will darken and become bitter if exposed to too much light.

WATERCRESS This has a tart, peppery taste, and is a member of the mustard family. Its strong flavour combines especially well with eggs, fish and grilled meats.

SALAD VEGETABLES The salad vegetable is any type that earns its keep in a salad by virtue of freshness and flavour. The list includes avocados, green beans, carrots, celery, cucumber, courgettes (zucchini), mushrooms, garlic, onions, spring onions (scallions), sweetcorn and tomatoes.

FRUIT The contents of the fruit bowl offers endless possibilities for sweet and savoury salads. Choose from apples, bananas, grapes, kiwis, lychees, mangoes, melons, oranges, papayas, pears, pineapples, raspberries, star fruit and strawberries, to name just a few.

SPICES Dried spices such as freshly ground black pepper, cayenne, cumin and ground coriander can add extra zing to salad dressings.

HERBS Fresh herbs bring character and flavour to salads and dressings. Basil, chives, coriander (cilantro), mint, parsley and thyme (below) are all very popular.

Preparing Salad Greens

LETTUCE
Discard wilted or damaged leaves.
Twist or cut out the central core.
Rinse the leaves thoroughly in cold
water and soak briefly to draw out any
grit trapped in the folds. Drain and
blot or spin dry. If the leaves are large,
tear into pieces.

ROCKET (ARUGULA)
Discard any wilted or damaged leaves.
Pull off any roots. Rinse thoroughly
and dry on kitchen paper – it's best
not to use a salad spinner, which
could bruise the tender leaves. Tear
rather than cut the leaves when using
in a salad.

LAMB'S LETTUCE
Remove any wilted or damaged leaves.
Trim the roots. Rinse well, as the
leaves can be sandy.

WATERCRESS
Discard wilted or damaged leaves and
snap off thick stalks. Rinse well and
spin dry.

Rinsing & Crisping Salad Greens

It is vital that all salad leaves be thoroughly rinsed with cold water to remove any grit or insects, as well as residues of chemical sprays. Just as important is to dry the salad leaves well so that the dressing will not be diluted. Careful drying will retain their crisp appearance.

1 Discard any wilted, discoloured or damaged leaves. For spinach and similar greens, pull off the stalks. Pull off roots from lamb's lettuce.

2 For leaves in compact or loose heads, pull them individually from the core or stalk.

3 Put the leaves in a sink or large basin of cold water and swirl them around to wash off any dirt or insects. Leave to settle for 1–2 minutes.

4 Lift the leaves out of the water. Drain briefly, then place them on a dish towel and pat dry gently with paper towels or another dish towel.

5 Alternatively, put the washed leaves in a salad spinner to spin off the water. (Do not, however, use a salad spinner for leaves that bruise easily.)

6 Wrap the leaves loosely in a clean dish towel or kitchen paper and put in a large plastic bag. Refrigerate for about 1 hour. When assembling the salad, tear any large leaves into smaller pieces.

SALAD SUCCESS
• Always use the finest and freshest ingredients with flavours that will complement each other.
• Dress salad greens just before serving, otherwise the leaves will wilt and become unpleasantly soggy.
• Match the dressing to the greens: sharp leaves need hearty flavours, but the same dressing used on the more delicate greens would overpower them.
• Be imaginative with salad additions. A few blanched green beans, for instance, can lift a plain salad, especially with a sprinkling of fresh herbs.

Salad Dressings

The best salad dressings are those that enhance the overall effect while still allowing the individual salad components to taste of themselves. It is therefore vital to choose the dressing ingredients carefully.

OLIVE OILS Extra virgin olive oil is made from the first cold pressing and is the finest quality. For dressings, French olive oils are the lightest, whereas Italian olive oils have a herby quality and Spanish olive oils are typically fruity. Greek olive oils have a strong flavour and colour that make them unsuitable for mayonnaise.

NUT OILS Hazelnut and walnut oils are usually blended with neutral oils for salad dressings.

SEED OILS Groundnut (peanut) oil and sunflower oil are chosen by many cooks for their clean, neutral flavour.

GARLIC OIL Garlic oil is made by steeping 4–5 crushed cloves of garlic in a neutral-flavoured oil.

VINEGARS White wine vinegar is the most popular type for salad dressings. It should be used in moderation to balance the richness of an oil.

LEMON AND LIME JUICE These juices impart a clean acidity to oil dressings. Like vinegar they should be used in moderation.

MUSTARD Where possible French, German and English mustards should be used for salads of the same nationality.

Below: A selection of oils, white wine vinegar and salad dressing flavourings.

Mayonnaise

Home-made mayonnaise is made with raw egg yolks and may therefore be considered unsuitable for young children, pregnant women and the elderly.

Makes about 300 ml/½ pint/ 1¼ cups

INGREDIENTS
2 egg yolks (at room temperature)
5 ml/1 tsp French mustard
150 ml/¼ pint/⅔ cup extra virgin olive oil
150 ml/¼ pint/⅔ cup groundnut or sunflower oil
10 ml/2 tsp white wine vinegar
salt and ground black pepper

1 Place the yolks and mustard in a food processor and blend smoothly.

2 Gradually add the olive oil, while the processor is running. When the mixture is thick, add the groundnut or sunflower oil in a slow stream. Add the vinegar and seasoning. It can be stored in the refrigerator for up to 1 week.

French Dressing

French vinaigrette is the most widely used salad dressing and is appreciated for its simplicity.

Makes about 120 ml/4 fl oz/ ½ cup

INGREDIENTS
90 ml/6 tbsp extra virgin olive oil
15 ml/1 tbsp white wine vinegar
5 ml/1 tsp French mustard
pinch of caster (superfine) sugar

1 Measure the extra virgin olive oil and white wine vinegar into a small screw-top jar.

2 Add the mustard and sugar. Replace the lid and shake well. Alternatively, whisk the dressing ingredients together, using a flat- bottomed whisk, in the salad bowl you are intending to use. Store at room temperature – not in the refrigerator – for up to 1 week.

Salade Niçoise

Salade Niçoise is a happy marriage of tuna fish, hard-boiled eggs, green beans and potatoes. Anchovies, olives and capers are often also included, but it is the first four ingredients that combine to make this a classic salad.

Serves 4

INGREDIENTS
675 g/1½ lb potatoes, peeled
225 g/8 oz green beans, topped
   and tailed
3 eggs, hard-boiled
1 cos lettuce
120 ml/4 fl oz/½ cup French Dressing
225 g/8 oz small plum tomatoes,
   cut into quarters
400 g/14 oz canned tuna steak in
   oil, drained
25 g/1 oz canned anchovy fillets, drained
30 ml/2 tbsp capers
12 black olives
salt and ground black pepper

1 Bring the potatoes to the boil in salted water and cook them for 20 minutes. Boil the green beans for 6 minutes. Drain and cool the potatoes and beans under running water.

2 If necessary, dry the potatoes with kitchen paper, then slice them thickly. Shell and quarter the eggs.

3 Wash the lettuce and spin dry, then chop the leaves roughly. Moisten the leaves with half of the dressing in a large salad bowl.

4 Moisten the potatoes, beans and tomatoes with the rest of the dressing, then scatter over the salad leaves.

5 Break up the tuna fish with a fork and distribute over the salad with the anchovy fillets, capers and olives. Season to taste and serve.

COOK'S TIP: The ingredients for Salade Niçoise can be prepared well in advance but should be assembled just before serving.

Caesar Salad

A classic salad that brings together the simplest ingredients.

Serves 6 as a starter

INGREDIENTS
175 ml/6 fl oz/¾ cup olive oil
75 g/3 oz French or Italian bread, cut into
    2.5 cm/1 in cubes
1 large garlic clove, crushed
2 small heads cos lettuce,
    separated into leaves,
    rinsed and crisped
2 eggs, boiled for 1 minute
75 ml/5 tbsp lemon juice
65 g/2½ oz/¾ cup Parmesan cheese,
    freshly grated
6 canned anchovy fillets, drained and
    roughly chopped
salt and ground black pepper

1 Heat 60 ml/4 tbsp of the oil in a frying pan. Add the bread cubes and garlic. Fry, stirring, until the cubes are golden brown. Drain on kitchen paper. Discard the garlic.

2 Put the lettuce into a large salad bowl, tearing any large leaves.

3 Add the remaining oil and season with salt and pepper. Toss the leaves.

4 Break the eggs on top, sprinkle with the lemon juice, then toss well again. Add the cheese and anchovies. Toss gently. Scatter the fried bread cubes on top and serve.

Cucumber & Fish Salad

A cool dish for summer – ideal served on individual plates for lunch.

Serves 4–8

INGREDIENTS

2 large cucumbers
500 g/1¼ lb fresh cod fillet,
    skinned
1 spring onion (scallion), finely
    chopped
small bunch of fresh dill
75 ml/5 tbsp milk
60 ml/4 tbsp mayonnaise
30 ml/2 tbsp crème fraîche or natural
    (plain) yogurt
175 g/6 oz/1½ cups cooked broad (fava)
    beans or peas
cucumber ribbons, to garnish
salt and ground black pepper

1 Peel one of the cucumbers and dice
the flesh. Remove six long, thin strips
from the other cucumber and then cut
the rest into dice. Sprinkle with salt
and leave to drain.

2 Poach the fish, spring onion, a few
sprigs of dill, the milk and seasoning
until the fish begins to flake. Lift it out
and leave to cool.

3 Wash the cucumber cubes and dry.
Mix the mayonnaise with the crème
fraîche or yogurt, stir in the cucumber,
broad beans or peas, then fold in the
fish. Serve, garnished with a few
cucumber ribbons.

Warm Salmon Salad

Light and fresh, this salad is perfect at any time of year. Serve it immediately, or you'll find the salad leaves will start to lose their bright colour and texture.

Serves 4

INGREDIENTS
450 g/1 lb salmon fillet, skinned
30 ml/2 tbsp sesame oil
grated rind (zest) of ½ orange
juice of 1 orange
5 ml/1 tsp Dijon mustard
15 ml/1 tbsp chopped fresh tarragon
45 ml/3 tbsp groundnut oil
115 g/4 oz fine green beans,
    trimmed
175 g/6 oz mixed salad leaves, such as young
    spinach leaves, radicchio, frisée and oak
    leaf lettuce
15 ml/1 tbsp sesame seeds, toasted
salt and ground black pepper

1 Cut the salmon into bite-size pieces, then make the dressing. Mix together the sesame oil, orange rind and juice, mustard, tarragon and seasoning in a bowl. Set aside.

2 Heat the groundnut oil in a frying pan. Add the salmon pieces and fry for 3–4 minutes, until lightly browned but still tender inside.

3 Blanch the green beans in boiling salted water for about 3–4 minutes, until tender yet crisp. Drain and rinse under cold running water. Drain the green beans again and pat dry with some kitchen paper.

4 Add the dressing to the salmon pieces, toss together gently and cook for 30 seconds. Remove the pan from the heat.

5 Arrange the prepared mixed salad leaves on serving plates. Toss the green beans over the leaves. Spoon over the salmon together with its cooking juices and serve immediately, sprinkled with the sesame seeds.

Thai Scented Fish Salad

For a tropical taste of the Far East, try this delicious and exotic fish salad.

Serves 4

INGREDIENTS
350 g/12 oz fillet of red mullet or sea bream
1 cos lettuce
½ lollo rosso lettuce
1 papaya or mango, peeled and sliced
1 pithaya or guava, peeled and sliced
1 large ripe tomato, cut into wedges
½ cucumber, peeled and cut into batons
3 spring onions (scallions), sliced

FOR THE MARINADE
5 ml/1 tsp coriander seeds
5 ml/1 tsp fennel seeds
2.5 ml/½ tsp cumin seeds
5 ml/1 tsp caster (superfine) sugar
2.5 ml/½ tsp hot chilli sauce
30 ml/2 tbsp garlic oil
2.5 ml/½ tsp salt

FOR THE DRESSING
15 ml/1 tbsp creamed coconut
60 ml/4 tbsp groundnut or safflower oil
finely grated rind (zest) and juice of 1 lime
1 red chilli, seeded and finely chopped
5 ml/1 tsp sugar
45 ml/3 tbsp chopped fresh coriander
   (cilantro)
2.5 ml/½ tsp salt

1 Cut the fish into strips and place in a shallow bowl. To make the marinade, crush the coriander, fennel and cumin seeds with the sugar. Mix in the chilli sauce, garlic oil and salt.

2 Spread the marinade over the fish, ensuring that it is well coated, cover and leave to stand in a cool place, or in the refrigerator, for at least 20 minutes – longer if time allows.

3 To make the dressing, place the creamed coconut and salt in a screw-top jar with 45 ml/3 tbsp boiling water and allow to dissolve. Add the groundnut or safflower oil, lime rind and juice, chopped red chilli, sugar and chopped fresh coriander. Shake well to combine thoroughly.

4 Wash and spin the lettuce leaves. Combine with the other salad vegetables. Toss with the dressing, then distribute between four large plates.

5 Heat a large non-stick frying pan, add the fish and cook for 5 minutes, turning once. Place the cooked fish over the salad and serve.

COOK'S TIP: If planning ahead, you can leave the fish in its marinade for up to 8 hours. The dressing can also be made in advance minus the fresh coriander. Store at room temperature and add the coriander when you are ready to assemble the salad.

Avocado, Crab & Coriander Salad

The sweet richness of fresh crab combines especially well with the flavours and colours of ripe avocado, fresh coriander (cilantro) and tomato.

Serves 4

INGREDIENTS
675 g/1½ lb small new potatoes
1 sprig fresh mint
900 g/2 lb boiled crabs
1 round (butterhead) lettuce
175 g/6 oz lamb's lettuce or young spinach
1 large ripe avocado, peeled and sliced
175 g/6 oz cherry tomatoes
salt, ground black pepper and nutmeg

FOR THE DRESSING
75 ml/5 tbsp olive oil
15 ml/1 tbsp lime juice
45 ml/3 tbsp chopped fresh coriander
    (cilantro)
½ tsp caster (superfine) sugar

2 Remove the legs and claws from each crab. Crack these open with the back of a chopping knife and then remove the white meat.

3 Turn the crab on its back and push the rear leg section away with the thumb and forefinger of each hand. Remove the soft brown meat from inside the shell.

4 Discard the soft gills ('dead men's fingers'): the crab uses these gills to filter impurities in its diet. Apart from these and the shell, everything else is edible – white and brown meat.

1 Boil the potatoes with the mint in salted water for 20 minutes, or until tender. Drain, cover and keep warm until needed.

5 Split the central body section open with a knife and remove the white and brown meat with a pick or skewer. Discard all the shells.

6 Combine the dressing ingredients in a screw-top jar and shake well to combine. Wash and spin the lettuces, then toss them in the dressing. Distribute the salad leaves among four plates. Top with avocado, crab, tomatoes and warm new potatoes. Season with salt, pepper and nutmeg and serve.

COOK'S TIP: Young crabs offer the sweetest meat. The hen crab carries more meat than the cock which has a better overall flavour. Some fishmongers sell fresh crab meat already extracted from the shell, or frozen crab meat is a good alternative.

Seafood Salad

Fabulous flavours of the sea are brought together in this attractive salad.

Serves 6

INGREDIENTS
115 g/4 oz prepared squid rings
1 large carrot
6 crisp lettuce leaves, torn into pieces
10 cm/4 in piece cucumber, finely diced
12 fresh mussels, in their shells, steamed
115 g/4 oz cooked, shelled prawns (shrimp)
15 ml/1 tbsp drained capers

FOR THE DRESSING
30 ml/2 tbsp lemon juice
45 ml/3 tbsp olive oil
15 ml/1 tbsp chopped fresh parsley
salt and ground black pepper

1 Put the squid rings in a metal strainer or vegetable steamer. Place over a saucepan of simmering water, cover and steam for 2–3 minutes, until the squid just turns white. Cool under cold running water and drain on kitchen paper.

2 Using a swivel-style vegetable peeler, cut the carrot into wafer-thin ribbons. Place the torn lettuce pieces on a serving plate. Scatter over the carrot ribbons, followed by the diced cucumber.

3 Arrange the mussels, prawns and squid rings over the salad on the serving plate and scatter with the drained capers.

4 Whisk the dressing ingredients together in a small bowl or shake in a screw-top jar. Drizzle over the seafood salad. Chill the salad before serving.

VARIATION: For a change, use any type of cooked seafood or fish in this salad – try steamed clams or cockles, prawns (shrimp) in their shells or cubes of firm white fish such as haddock or halibut.

Grilled Chicken Salad with Lavender

Lavender may seem like an odd salad ingredient, but its delightful scent has a natural affinity with sweet garlic, orange and other wild herbs.

Serves 4

INGREDIENTS
4 boneless chicken breasts
900 ml/1½ pints/3¾ cups light
   chicken stock
175 g/6 oz/1½ cups fine polenta
   or cornmeal
50 g/2 oz/4 tbsp butter
450 g/1 lb young spinach
175 g/6 oz lamb's lettuce
salt and ground black pepper
8 sprigs fresh lavender, to garnish
8 small tomatoes, halved, to garnish

FOR THE LAVENDER MARINADE
6 fresh lavender flowers
10 ml/2 tsp finely grated
   orange rind
2 garlic cloves, crushed
10 ml/2 tsp clear honey
30 ml/2 tbsp olive oil
10 ml/2 tsp chopped fresh thyme
10 ml/2 tsp chopped fresh marjoram

1 To make the marinade, strip the lavender flowers from the stems and combine with the orange rind, garlic, honey and some salt. Add the olive oil and herbs. Slash the chicken breasts deeply, spread the mixture over the chicken and leave to marinate for at least 20 minutes.

2 To prepare the polenta, bring the chicken stock to the boil in a saucepan. Add the polenta or cornmeal in a steady stream, stirring, until thick: this will take 2–3 minutes. Turn the polenta out on to a 2.5 cm/1 in deep buttered tray and allow to cool.

3 Preheat the grill (broiler) to a moderate temperature. Grill (broil) the chicken for approximately 15 minutes, turning once.

4 When the polenta is cool and firm cut it into 2.5 cm/1 in cubes with a sharp wet knife. Heat the butter gently in a large, heavy-based frying pan and fry the polenta over a moderate heat, turning once until golden brown in appearance.

5 Wash the salad leaves and spin dry, then divide between four large plates. Slice each chicken breast and lay over the salad. Place the polenta among the salad, garnish with sprigs of fresh lavender and halved tomatoes, season and serve.

Warm Chicken Salad

This salad needs to be served warm to make the most of the wonderful sesame and herby flavourings.

Serves 6

INGREDIENTS
4 medium boneless chicken breasts, skinned
225 g/8 oz mangetouts (snow peas)
2 heads lollo rosso or oak leaf lettuce
3 carrots, peeled and cut into matchsticks
175 g/6 oz/2⅓ cups button (white)
   mushrooms, sliced
6 bacon slices, fried and chopped
fresh coriander (cilantro) leaves, to garnish

FOR THE DRESSING
120 ml/4 fl oz/½ cup lemon juice
30 ml/2 tbsp wholegrain mustard
250 ml/8 fl oz/1 cup olive oil
65 ml/2½ fl oz/⅓ cup sesame oil
5 ml/1 tsp coriander seeds, crushed

1 Mix all the dressing ingredients in a bowl. Put the chicken in a shallow dish and pour on half of the dressing. Marinate in the refrigerator overnight.

2 Cook the mangetouts in boiling water for 2 minutes, then cool under cold running water. Tear the lettuces into small pieces and mix with the other vegetables and the bacon. Arrange in individual serving dishes.

3 Grill the chicken until cooked through, then slice thinly on the diagonal. Divide between the bowls of salad and add some dressing to each one. Combine quickly, garnish with fresh coriander and serve.

Chicken Liver & Bacon Salad

This rich, warm salad with sweet spinach, tomatoes and bitter leaves of frisée lettuce will brighten autumn days.

Serves 4

INGREDIENTS
225 g/8 oz young spinach leaves,
    stems removed
1 frisée lettuce
6 slices rindless unsmoked bacon,
    cut into strips
105 ml/7 tbsp groundnut or sunflower oil
75 g/3 oz day-old bread, crusts removed
    and cut into short fingers
450 g/1 lb chicken livers
115 g/4 oz cherry tomatoes
salt and ground black pepper

1 Wash and spin the salad leaves. Place in a salad bowl, tearing any which are large.

2 Fry the bacon in 60 ml/4 tbsp of the oil for 3–4 minutes, or until crisp and brown. Remove the bacon with a slotted spoon and drain on kitchen paper. Keep warm.

3 To make the croûtons, fry the bread in the bacon-flavoured oil, stirring and turning constantly until crisp and golden brown all over. Drain on kitchen paper.

4 Heat the remaining 45 ml/3 tbsp of the oil, add the chicken livers and fry briskly for 2–3 minutes. Turn the livers out over the salad leaves, add the bacon, croûtons and tomatoes. Season, toss and serve.

Warm Duck Salad with Orange & Coriander

The rich, gamey flavour of duck provides the foundation for this delicious salad, ideal for cooler seasons of the year.

Serves 4

INGREDIENTS

1 small orange
2 boneless duck breasts
150 ml/¼ pint/⅔ cup dry white wine
5 ml/1 tsp ground coriander
2.5 ml/½ tsp ground cumin or fennel seeds
30 ml/2 tbsp caster (superfine) sugar
juice of ½ small lime or lemon
75 g/3 oz day-old bread, crusts removed and cut into short fingers
45 ml/3 tbsp garlic oil
½ escarole lettuce
½ frisée lettuce
30 ml/2 tbsp sunflower or groundnut oil
salt and cayenne pepper
4 sprigs fresh coriander (cilantro), to garnish

1 Halve the orange and slice each half thickly. Simmer in water for 5 minutes. Drain and set aside.

2 Pierce the skin of the duck breasts and rub with salt. Place a heavy frying pan over a steady heat and dry-fry the breasts for 20 minutes, turning once, until they are medium-rare.

3 Transfer to a warm plate, cover and keep warm. Pour the duck fat into a small bowl and set aside for use on another occasion.

4 Heat the sediment in the frying pan until it begins to darken. Add the white wine and stir to loosen the sediment. Add the ground coriander, cumin or fennel, sugar and orange slices. Boil quickly and reduce to a coating consistency.

5 Sharpen with lime or lemon juice and season to taste with salt and cayenne pepper. Transfer to a bowl, cover and keep warm.

6 To make the croûtons, fry the bread in the garlic oil until evenly crisp. Season with salt, then drain on kitchen paper.

7 Wash and spin the salad leaves. Moisten with sunflower or groundnut oil and distribute between four large serving plates.

8 Slice the duck breasts diagonally and divide among the salad plates along with the orange slices. Spoon on the dressing, scatter with croûtons, garnish with fresh coriander and serve.

COOK'S TIP: Duck breast has the quality of red meat and is cooked either rare, medium or well done according to taste.

Frisée Salad with Bacon

A classic French salad that combines different flavours and textures.
It can be served as a starter or light lunch.

Serves 4

INGREDIENTS
225 g/8 oz frisée or escarole leaves
75–90 ml/5–6 tbsp extra virgin olive oil
175 g/6 oz piece smoked bacon, diced, or
   6 thick-cut smoked bacon slices,
   cut crossways into thin strips
50 g/2 oz/1 cup white bread cubes
1 small garlic clove, finely chopped
15 ml/1 tbsp red wine vinegar
10 ml/2 tsp Dijon mustard
salt and ground black pepper

1 Wash and spin the salad leaves.
Tear into bite-size pieces and put in a
salad bowl.

2 Heat 15 ml/1 tbsp of the oil in a
non-stick frying pan over a medium-
low heat and add the bacon pieces.
Fry gently until well browned, stirring
occasionally. Remove the bacon with a
slotted spoon and drain on kitchen
paper. Keep warm.

3 Add another 30 ml/2 tbsp of the
oil to the pan and fry the bread cubes
over a medium–high heat, turning
frequently, until evenly browned.
Remove the bread cubes with a
slotted spoon and drain on kitchen
paper. Discard any fat remaining in
the pan.

4 Stir the chopped garlic, red wine
vinegar and mustard into the pan with
the remaining olive oil and heat the
mixture until just warm, whisking to
combine. Season to taste, then pour
the dressing over the salad leaves and
sprinkle with the fried bacon pieces
and the croûtons.

VARIATION: For a country-style
salad, dandelion leaves can replace
the frisée and chopped hard-boiled
egg can be sprinkled over the top to
make it more substantial.

Mushroom Salad with Parma Ham

An irresistible, warming salad to make in autumn when a wonderful variety of wild mushrooms are available.

Serves 4

INGREDIENTS
40 g/1½ oz/3 tbsp unsalted butter
175 g/6 oz Parma ham, thickly sliced
450 g/1 lb assorted wild and cultivated
    mushrooms such as chanterelles, ceps
    (porcini), bay boletus, Caesar's
    mushrooms, oyster and field (portabello),
    trimmed and sliced
60 ml/4 tbsp Madeira or sherry
juice of ½ lemon
½ oak leaf lettuce
½ frisée lettuce
30 ml/2 tbsp walnut oil

FOR THE PANCAKE RIBBONS
25 g/1 oz/¼ cup plain (all-purpose) flour
75 ml/5 tbsp milk
1 egg
60 ml/4 tbsp freshly grated Parmesan cheese
60 ml/4 tbsp chopped fresh herbs, such as
    parsley, thyme, marjoram or chives
salt and ground black pepper

1 To make the pancakes, blend the flour and the milk. Beat in the egg, cheese, herbs and seasoning. Heat a little of the butter in a frying pan and pour enough of the mixture into the pan to coat the bottom. When the batter has set, turn the pancake over and cook briefly on the other side.

2 Turn out the pancake and cool. Roll it up and slice thinly to make 1 cm/½ in ribbons. Cook the remaining batter in the same way. Cut the ham into similar-size ribbons and toss with the pancake ribbons.

3 Gently soften the various types of mushroom in the remaining butter for 6–8 minutes, until the moisture has evaporated. Add the Madeira or sherry, lemon juice and salt and pepper to taste.

4 Toss the salad leaves in the oil and arrange on four plates. Place the ham and pancake ribbons in the centre, spoon on the mushrooms and serve warm.

VARIATION: Finely grate some carrot and add to the batter in place of the herbs.

Prosciutto Salad with an Avocado Fan

Feast on this elegant salad, a showcase for the versatile avocado. Prosciutto and avocado make ideal partners in this impressive but simple dish.

Serves 4

INGREDIENTS
3 avocados
150 g/5 oz prosciutto
75–115 g/3–4 oz rocket (arugula)
24 marinated black olives,
    drained

FOR THE DRESSING
15 ml/1 tbsp balsamic vinegar
5 ml/1 tsp lemon juice
5 ml/1 tsp English mustard
5 ml/1 tsp sugar
75 ml/5 tbsp olive oil
salt and ground black pepper

1 To make the dressing, combine the vinegar, lemon juice, mustard and sugar in a bowl. Whisk in the oil, a little at a time, season with salt and pepper and set aside.

2 Cut 2 of the avocados in half. Remove the stones and skin, and cut the flesh into 1 cm/½ in slices. Toss with half of the dressing. Place the prosciutto, avocado and rocket on four plates. Sprinkle the olives and the remaining dressing over the salads.

3 Halve, stone and peel the remaining avocado. Slice each half lengthways into quarters. Gently draw a cannelle knife across the avocado quarters at 1 cm/½ in intervals, to create indentations in a regular striped pattern across the avocado.

4 Make four cuts lengthways down each avocado quarter, leaving 1 cm/ ½ in intact at the end. Carefully fan out the slices, arrange on the plates, to one side of the other salad ingredients, and serve immediately.

Rocket & Grilled Goat's Cheese Salad

For this recipe, look out for cylinder-shaped goat's cheese from a delicatessen or for small rolls that can be cut into halves weighing about 50 g/2 oz. This salad could also serve four as a starter.

Serves 2

INGREDIENTS
about 15 ml/1 tbsp olive oil
about 15 ml/1 tbsp vegetable oil
4 slices French bread
45 ml/3 tbsp walnut oil
15 ml/1 tbsp lemon juice
225 g/8 oz cylinder-shaped
   goat's cheese
generous handful rocket (arugula) leaves
generous handful frisée lettuce
salt and ground black pepper

FOR THE SAUCE
45 ml/3 tbsp apricot jam
60 ml/4 tbsp white wine
5 ml/1 tsp Dijon mustard

1 Heat the olive and vegetable oils in a frying pan and fry the slices of French bread on one side only, until lightly golden. Transfer to a plate lined with kitchen paper.

2 To make the sauce, heat the jam in a small saucepan until warm but not boiling. Push through a strainer, into a clean pan, to remove the pieces of fruit, and then stir in the white wine and mustard. Heat gently and keep warm until ready to serve.

3 Blend together the walnut oil and lemon juice and season with a little salt and ground black pepper. Stir well and set aside.

4 Preheat the grill (broiler) a few minutes before serving the salad. Cut the goat's cheese into 50 g/2 oz rounds and put each piece on a croûton, untoasted side up. Place under the hot grill and cook for 3–4 minutes, until the cheese melts and begins to bubble.

5 Toss the rocket and frisée leaves in the walnut oil dressing and arrange on two individual serving plates. When the cheese croûtons are ready, arrange two on each plate on top of the salad and pour over a little of the apricot sauce.

Parmesan & Poached Egg Salad with Croûtons

Soft poached eggs, hot garlic croûtons and cool, crisp salad leaves make an unforgettable combination in this tasty salad.

Serves 2

INGREDIENTS
½ small loaf white bread
75 ml/5 tbsp extra virgin olive oil
2 eggs
115 g/4 oz mixed salad leaves
2 garlic cloves, crushed
7.5 ml/1½ tsp white wine vinegar
25 g/1 oz/⅓ cup Parmesan cheese shavings
ground black pepper

1 Remove the crust from the bread. Cut the bread into 2.5 cm/1 in cubes. Heat 30 ml/2 tbsp of the oil in a frying pan and cook the bread for about 5 minutes, tossing the cubes occasionally, until they are golden brown all over.

2 Meanwhile, bring a pan of water to the boil. Break the eggs and slide in, one at a time. Gently poach the eggs for 4 minutes, until lightly cooked.

3 Divide the salad leaves between two plates. Remove the croûtons from the pan and arrange them over the leaves. Wipe the pan clean with kitchen paper.

4 Heat the remaining oil in the pan, add the garlic and white wine vinegar and cook over high heat for just 1 minute. Pour the warm dressing over each salad.

5 Place a poached egg on each dressed salad. Scatter with shavings of Parmesan cheese and a little freshly ground black pepper.

COOK'S TIP: When poaching eggs, a dash of vinegar in the water will keep the whites together. Swirl the water using a spoon before sliding in the egg.

Bountiful Bean Salad

This delicious, filling salad, brimming with contrasting flavours and textures, keeps well in the refrigerator and can be made up to 3 days in advance.

Serves 6

INGREDIENTS
75 g/3 oz/½ cup red kidney, pinto or
   borlotti beans
75 g/3 oz/½ cup white cannellini or
   butter (lima) beans
30 ml/2 tbsp olive oil
175 g/6 oz cut fresh green beans
3 spring onions (scallions), sliced
1 small yellow or red (bell) pepper, seeded
   and sliced
1 carrot, coarsely grated
30 ml/2 tbsp sun-dried tomatoes,
   chopped
50 g/2 oz/½ cup unsalted cashew nuts or
   almonds, split

FOR THE DRESSING
45 ml/3 tbsp sunflower oil
30 ml/2 tbsp red wine vinegar
15 ml/1 tbsp coarse grain mustard
5 ml/1 tsp caster (superfine) sugar
5 ml/1 tsp dried mixed herbs
salt and ground black pepper

1 Soak the dried beans, overnight if possible, then drain and rinse well. Cover with plenty of cold water and fast boil for 10 minutes, then simmer until tender.

2 When cooked, drain and season the beans and toss them in the olive oil. Leave to cool for 30 minutes.

3 In a large bowl, mix the beans with all the other vegetables, including the sun-dried tomatoes but not the cashew nuts or almonds.

4 To make the dressing, shake all the ingredients together in a screw-top jar until well blended. Toss the dressing into the bean salad and check the seasoning. Serve sprinkled with the split cashew nuts or almonds.

Roast Pepper & Wild Mushroom Pasta Salad

A combination of grilled (bell) peppers and wild mushrooms makes this pasta salad colourful as well as nutritious.

Serves 6

INGREDIENTS
1 red (bell) pepper, halved
1 yellow (bell) pepper, halved
1 green (bell) pepper, halved
350 g/12 oz/3 cups wholewheat pasta
  shells or twists
30 ml/2 tbsp olive oil
45 ml/3 tbsp balsamic vinegar
75 ml/5 tbsp tomato juice
30 ml/2 tbsp chopped fresh basil
15 ml/1 tbsp chopped
  fresh thyme
175 g/6 oz/2⅓ cups shiitake
  mushrooms, sliced
175 g/6 oz/2⅓ cups oyster
  mushrooms, sliced
400 g/14 oz can black-eyed beans, rinsed
  and drained
115 g/4 oz/⅔ cup sultanas (golden raisins)
2 bunches of spring onions (scallions),
  finely chopped
salt and ground black pepper

VARIATION: This salad works equally well with any kind of pasta shapes such as farfalle or penne. You could also use different mushrooms such as fresh ceps (porcini) instead of shiitake.

1 Preheat the grill (broiler). Put the peppers cut-side down on a grill (broiling) pan rack and place under a hot grill for 10–15 minutes, until the skins are charred. Cover the peppers with a clean, damp dish towel and set aside to cool.

2 Meanwhile, cook the pasta in lightly salted, boiling water for 10–12 minutes until *al dente*. Drain.

3 Mix together the oil, vinegar, tomato juice, basil and thyme, add to the warm pasta and toss together.

4 Remove and carefully peel the skins from the peppers and discard. Seed and slice the peppers and add to the pasta with the mushrooms, beans, sultanas, spring onions and seasoning. Toss the ingredients to mix and serve immediately or cover and chill in the refrigerator before serving.

Thai Noodle Salad

The addition of coconut milk and sesame oil gives an unusual, nutty flavour to the dressing for this colourful noodle salad.

Serves 4–6

INGREDIENTS
350 g/12 oz somen noodles
1 large carrot, cut into thin strips
1 bunch asparagus, trimmed and cut
    into 4 cm/1½ in lengths
1 red (bell) pepper, cut into fine strips
115 g/4 oz mangetouts (snow peas), topped,
    tailed and halved
115 g/4 oz baby corn cobs, halved
    lengthways
115 g/4 oz/½ cup beansprouts
115 g/4 oz can water chestnuts, drained
    and finely sliced
1 lime, cut into wedges, 50 g/2 oz/½ cup
    roasted peanuts, roughly chopped, and
    fresh coriander (cilantro) leaves, to garnish

FOR THE DRESSING
45 ml/3 tbsp roughly torn fresh basil
75 ml/5 tbsp roughly chopped fresh mint
250 ml/8 fl oz/1 cup coconut milk
30 ml/2 tbsp dark sesame oil
15 ml/1 tbsp grated fresh root ginger
2 garlic cloves, finely chopped
juice of 1 lime
2 spring onions (scallions), finely chopped
salt and cayenne pepper

1 To make the dressing, combine all the ingredients in a bowl and mix well. Season to taste with salt and cayenne pepper.

2 Cook the noodles in a saucepan of boiling water until just tender, following the directions on the packet. Drain, rinse under cold running water and drain again.

3 Cook all the vegetables separately in boiling, lightly salted water until tender but still crisp. Alternatively, lightly steam the vegetables in batches. Drain, plunge them immediately into cold water and drain again.

4 Toss the noodles, vegetables and dressing together to combine. Arrange on individual serving plates and garnish with the lime wedges, peanuts and coriander leaves.

VARIATION: Shredded omelette or sliced hard–boiled eggs can be used as alternative garnishes. Or add tuna for non–vegetarians.

Gado Gado

The peanut sauce is served separately from this salad and everyone helps themselves. Prawn crackers may also be included for non-vegetarians.

Serves 4–6

INGREDIENTS
2 medium potatoes, peeled
175 g/6 oz green beans, topped
    and tailed
175 g/6 oz/1½ cups Chinese
    leaves, shredded
1 iceberg lettuce
175 g/6 oz/¾ cup beansprouts
½ cucumber, cut into fingers
150 g/5 oz/1 cup giant white
    radish, shredded
3 spring onions (scallions)
225 g/8 oz firm tofu, rinsed,
    drained and cut into large dice
3 hard-boiled eggs, quartered

FOR THE PEANUT SAUCE
150 g/5 oz/¾ cup raw peanuts
15 ml/1 tbsp vegetable oil
2 shallots or 1 small onion, finely chopped
1 garlic clove, crushed
1–2 small chillies, seeded and
    finely chopped
30 ml/2 tbsp tamarind sauce
120 ml/4 fl oz/½ cup canned
    coconut milk
15 ml/1 tbsp clear honey

1 Bring the potatoes to the boil in salted water and simmer them for 20 minutes. Meanwhile cook the beans for 3–4 minutes. Drain both and refresh under cold running water.

2 To make the peanut sauce, dry-fry the peanuts in a wok, or place under a moderate preheated grill (broiler), tossing them all the time to prevent burning. Turn the peanuts on to a clean cloth and rub vigorously with your hands to remove the papery skins. Place the peanuts in a food processor and blend for 2 minutes.

3 Heat the oil in a wok, and soften the shallots or onion, garlic and chillies, gently, without letting them colour. Add the tamarind sauce, coconut milk and honey. Simmer briefly, add to the peanuts and process to form a thick sauce.

4 Spoon the sauce into a serving bowl and place on a large serving platter. Arrange the cooked potatoes, prepared beans and all the remaining salad ingredients in groups around the peanut sauce. Serve hot.

Mixed Green Salad

Include distinctively flavoured leaves and herbs when you make this salad.

Serves 4–6

INGREDIENTS
1 garlic clove
30 ml/2 tbsp red wine or sherry vinegar
5 ml/1 tsp Dijon mustard (optional)
75–120 ml/5–8 tbsp extra virgin olive oil
200–225 g/7–8 oz mixed salad leaves
    and herbs
salt and ground black pepper

1 Peel the garlic clove. Rub a large salad bowl with the garlic clove and leave in the bowl.

2 Add the vinegar, salt and pepper and mustard, if using. Stir to mix the ingredients and dissolve the salt, then slowly whisk in the oil.

3 Wash and spin the salad leaves and herbs. Remove the garlic clove from the bowl and stir the vinaigrette to combine. Add the salad leaves and herbs to the bowl and toss well. Serve the salad at once.

VARIATION: This salad benefits from the addition of some pungent leaves, such as dandelion or sorrel when in season.

Apple & Celeriac Salad

Celeriac, despite its coarse appearance, has a sweet and subtle flavour.

Serves 3–4

INGREDIENTS
675 g/1½ lb celeriac, peeled
10–15 ml/2–3 tsp lemon juice
5 ml/1 tsp walnut oil (optional)
1 apple
45 ml/3 tbsp mayonnaise
10 ml/2 tsp Dijon mustard
15 ml/1 tbsp chopped fresh parsley
salt and ground black pepper

1 Using a food processor or coarse cheese grater, shred the celeriac. Alternatively, cut it into very thin julienne strips. Place the celeriac in a bowl and mix in the lemon juice and the walnut oil, if using.

2 Peel the apple, if you like, cut it into quarters and remove the core. Slice thinly crossways and toss thoroughly with the celeriac.

3 Mix together the mayonnaise, mustard, parsley and salt and pepper to taste. Stir into the celeriac mixture and mix well. Chill for several hours until ready to serve.

Right: Mixed Green Salad (top); Apple & Celeriac Salad

Carrot, Raisin & Apricot Coleslaw

The light yogurt dressing complements the crisp textures in this coleslaw.

Serves 6

INGREDIENTS
350 g/12 oz/3 cups white cabbage,
    finely shredded
225 g/8 oz/1½ cups carrots,
    coarsely grated
1 red onion, sliced
3 celery sticks, sliced
175 g/6 oz/1 cup raisins
75 g/3 oz/⅓ cup ready-to-eat dried apricots
    or pears, chopped
120 ml/4 fl oz/½ cup mayonnaise
90 ml/6 tbsp natural (plain) yogurt
30 ml/2 tbsp chopped fresh
    mixed herbs
salt and ground black pepper

1 Put the cabbage and carrot in a large bowl. Add the onion, celery, raisins and apricots or pears and mix well.

2 In a small bowl, mix together the mayonnaise, yogurt, herbs and salt and pepper to taste.

3 Add the mayonnaise dressing to the salad and toss the ingredients together to mix. Cover and chill for several hours before serving.

VARIATION: Use other dried fruit such as chopped dates or peaches.

Mixed Vegetable Salad

This tasty, colourful dish is also known as Russian Salad.

Serves 4

INGREDIENTS
8 new potatoes, scrubbed and quartered
1 large carrot, diced
115 g/4 oz fine green beans, cut into 2 cm/
    ¾ in lengths
75 g/3 oz/¾ cup peas
½ onion, chopped
4 cornichons or small gherkins, sliced
1 small red (bell) pepper, seeded and diced
50 g/2 oz/½ cup pitted black olives
15 ml/1 tbsp capers
60–90 ml/4–6 tbsp aïoli or mayonnaise
15 ml/1 tbsp lemon juice
45 ml/3 tbsp chopped fresh dill
salt and ground black pepper

1 Cook the potatoes and carrot in boiling, lightly salted water until almost tender. Add the beans and peas and cook until all the vegetables are tender. Drain.

2 Tip the cooked vegetables into a large bowl. Mix in the onion, cornichons or gherkins, red pepper, olives and capers. Stir the aïoli or mayonnaise and lemon juice together.

3 Add most of the dressing and 30 ml/2 tbsp dill to the vegetables and season. Toss well. Chill until ready to serve, then drizzle with the remaining dressing and garnish with dill.

New Potato Salad

A wonderful salad to make with the season's new potatoes.

Serves 6

INGREDIENTS
900 g/2 lb baby new potatoes
2 green apples
4 spring onions (scallions)
3 celery sticks, finely chopped
150 ml/¼ pint/⅔ cup mayonnaise
salt and ground black pepper

1 Cook the potatoes in boiling, lightly salted water for about 20 minutes, or until just tender.

2 Core and chop the apples. Clean and chop the spring onions and celery quite finely.

3 Drain the potatoes well and immediately add all the other ingredients. Season to taste and stir until well mixed. Leave to cool and serve cold.

French Bean Salad

The secret of this recipe is to dress the beans while they are still hot.

Serves 6

INGREDIENTS
175 g/6 oz cherry tomatoes, halved
5 ml/1 tsp sugar
450 g/1 lb green beans, topped and tailed
175 g/6 oz feta cheese, cut into chunks
salt and ground black pepper

FOR THE DRESSING
90 ml/6 tbsp olive oil
45 ml/3 tbsp white wine vinegar
1.5 ml/¼ tsp Dijon mustard
2 garlic cloves, crushed

1 Preheat the oven to 230°C/450°F/ Gas 8. Put the cherry tomatoes on a baking sheet and sprinkle over the sugar, salt and pepper. Roast for 20 minutes, then leave to cool. Meanwhile, cook the beans in boiling, lightly salted water for 10 minutes, or until just tender.

2 Whisk together the oil, vinegar, mustard, garlic and seasoning to taste. Drain the beans and immediately pour over the vinaigrette and mix well. When cool, stir in the tomatoes and the feta cheese. Serve chilled.

Right: New Potato Salad (top); French Bean Salad

Fruity Brown Rice Salad

An Oriental-style dressing gives this colourful rice salad extra piquancy.

Serves 4–6

INGREDIENTS
115 g/4 oz/⅔ cup brown rice
4 spring onions (scallions), to garnish
1 small red (bell) pepper, seeded and diced
200 g/7 oz can sweetcorn
 (corn), drained
45 ml/3 tbsp sultanas (golden raisins)
225 g/8 oz can pineapple pieces in
 fruit juice
15 ml/1 tbsp light soy sauce
15 ml/1 tbsp sunflower oil
15 ml/1 tbsp hazelnut oil
1 garlic clove, crushed
5 ml/1 tsp finely chopped fresh
 root ginger
salt and freshly ground black pepper

1 Cook the brown rice in a large saucepan of boiling, lightly salted water for about 30 minutes, or until it is tender. Drain thoroughly and cool. Meanwhile, prepare the garnish by slicing the spring onions at an angle; set aside.

2 Tip the rice into a bowl and add the red pepper, sweetcorn and sultanas. Drain the pineapple pieces, reserving the juice, then add them to the rice mixture and toss lightly.

3 Pour the reserved pineapple juice into a clean screw-top jar. Add the soy sauce, sunflower and hazelnut oils, garlic, root ginger, salt and pepper. Then close the jar tightly and shake well to combine.

VARIATION: You can use other ingredients for this salad. Try lightly steamed broccoli or cauliflower florets, or sliced water chestnuts. It could be made more substantial by adding some toasted cashew nut pieces and a can of drained red kidney beans.

4 Pour the dressing over the salad and toss well. Cover with clear film (plastic wrap) and chill untill needed but allow the salad to stand for 20 minutes before serving with the spring onions scattered over the top.

Tabbouleh with Fennel & Pomegranate

A fresh salad originating in the Middle East, with the added crunchiness of fennel and sweet pomegranate seeds. It is perfect for a summer lunch.

Serves 6

INGREDIENTS
225 g/8 oz/1⅓ cups bulgur wheat
2 fennel bulbs
1 small red chilli
1 celery stick
30 ml/2 tbsp olive oil
finely grated rind (zest) and juice of 2
　　lemons
6–8 spring onions (scallions), chopped
90 ml/6 tbsp chopped fresh mint
90 ml/6 tbsp chopped fresh parsley
1 pomegranate, seeds separated
salt and freshly ground black pepper

3 Trim and halve the fennel bulbs and cut into very fine slices. Carefully seed and finely chop the chilli. Finely slice the celery.

1 Place the bulgur wheat in a bowl cover with cold water. Leave to absorb the liquid for 30 minutes.

2 Drain the wheat through a strainer placed over a bowl, pressing out any excess water using a spoon.

4 Mix all the salad ingredients together, including the soaked bulgur wheat. (Make sure all the bitter pith is removed from around the flesh of the pomegranate seeds.) Season well, cover and set aside for 30 minutes before serving.

Iced Pineapple Crush with Strawberries & Lychees

The sweet, tropical flavours of pineapple and lychees combine well with richly scented strawberries to make this a most refreshing salad.

Serves 4

INGREDIENTS
2 small pineapples
450 g/1 lb/4 cups strawberries
400 g/14 oz can lychees, drained
45 ml/3 tbsp kirsch or white rum
30 ml/2 tbsp icing (confectioners') sugar

1 Remove the crown from both pineapples by twisting sharply. Reserve the leaves for decoration.

2 Cut the fruit in half diagonally with a large, serrated knife. Cut around the flesh inside the skin with a small, serrated knife, keeping the skin intact. Remove the core.

VARIATION: Try replacing the lychees with fresh mango, cut into chunks: heavenly!

3 Chop the pineapple flesh and gently combine with the strawberries and lychees, taking care not to damage the fruit.

4 Combine the kirsch or white rum with the icing sugar. Pour over the fruit, toss gently and place in the freezer for 45 minutes.

5 Turn the fruit out into the pineapple skins and decorate with pineapple leaves. Serve immediately.

Exotic Fruit Salad

Passion fruit dressing brings out the flavours of this exotic fruit salad.

Serves 6

INGREDIENTS
1 mango
1 papaya
2 kiwi fruit
coconut or vanilla ice cream, to serve

FOR THE DRESSING
3 passion fruit
thinly pared rind (zest) and juice of 1 lime
5 ml/1 tsp hazelnut or walnut oil
15 ml/1 tbsp clear honey

1 Peel the mango, cut it into three slices, then cut the flesh into chunks and place it in a large bowl. Peel the papaya and cut it in half. Remove the seeds and chop the flesh.

2 Cut both ends off each kiwi fruit, then stand them on a board. Using a small, sharp knife, cut off the skin from top to bottom. Cut each kiwi fruit in half lengthways, then cut into thick slices. Combine all the fruit in a large bowl.

3 To make the dressing, cut each passion fruit in half and scoop out the seeds into a strainer set over a bowl. Press the seeds to extract all their juices. Lightly whisk the dressing ingredients into the passion fruit juice.

4 Pour the dressing over the fruit and mix gently to combine. Leave to chill for 1 hour before serving with scoops of ice cream.

Emerald Fruit Salad

A jewel–like medley of sumptuous fruits that lives up to its name.

Serves 4

INGREDIENTS
30 ml/2 tbsp lime juice
30 ml/2 tbsp clear honey
2 green eating apples, cored
    and sliced
1 small ripe Ogen melon, diced
2 kiwi fruit, sliced
1 star fruit, sliced
mint sprigs, to decorate
natural (plain) yogurt or fromage frais,
    to serve

1 Using a whisk, mix together the lime juice and honey in a large bowl, then toss the apple slices into the marinade, making sure the apple slices are thoroughly coated.

2 Stir in the melon, kiwi fruit and star fruit. Place in a glass serving dish and chill before serving.

3 Decorate the fruit salad with mint sprigs and serve with natural yogurt or fromage frais.

Summer Red Fruit Salad

This salad can be prepared the day before serving.

Serves 8

INGREDIENTS
225 g/8 oz/1⅓ cups raspberries
   or blackberries
50 g/2 oz/½ cup redcurrants
   or blackcurrants
30–60 ml/2–4 tbsp caster (superfine) sugar
8 ripe plums, stoned and sliced
8 ripe apricots, stoned and sliced
225 g/8 oz/1 cup seedless grapes
115 g/4 oz/1 cup strawberries

1 Put the berries and currants in a pan with 30 ml/2 tbsp sugar. Add half of the plum and apricot slices.

2 Cook over a very low heat with about 45 ml/3 tbsp water until the fruit is just beginning to soften and the juices are starting to run. Alternatively, cook in a bowl with no water, in the microwave.

3 Leave to cool slightly and then add the remaining sliced plums and apricots, and the grapes. Taste and add more sugar if necessary. Leave to cool, cover and chill.

4 Just before serving, transfer the fruit to a serving bowl. Slice the strawberries and arrange them on top.

Watermelon & Grapefruit Salad

This pretty, pink combination is light and refreshing for any summer meal.

Serves 4

INGREDIENTS
500 g/1¼ lb/2 cups diced watermelon flesh
2 ruby or pink grapefruit
2 pieces stem ginger in syrup
30 ml/2 tbsp stem ginger syrup

1 Remove any seeds from the watermelon and discard them. Cut the flesh into bite-size cubes.

2 Using a small, sharp knife, cut away all the peel and white pith from the grapefruit and carefully lift out the segments, catching any juice in a bowl.

3 Finely chop the stem ginger and place in a serving bowl with the watermelon cubes and the grapefruit segments, adding the reserved juice from the grapefruit.

4 Spoon over the stem ginger syrup and toss the fruits together lightly to ensure they are evenly coated. Chill the salad before serving.

COOK'S TIP: Toss the fruits gently grapefruit segments will break up easily and the appearance of the dish will be spoiled.

Index

This edition is published by Lorenz Books,
an imprint of Anness Publishing Ltd,
108 Great Russell Street, London WC1B 3NA info@anness.com

www.lorenzbooks.com; www.annesspublishing.com

© Anness Publishing Limited 2014

If you like the images in this book and would like to investigate
using them for publishing, promotions or advertising, please visit
our website www.practicalpictures.com for more information.

Publisher: Joanna Lorenz
Editor: Valerie Ferguson & Helen Sudell
Series Designer: Bobbie Colgate Stone
Designer: Andrew Heath
Production Controller: Steve Lang

Recipes contributed by: Angela Boggiano,
Janet Brinkworth, Kit Chan, Carole Clements,
Matthew Drennan, Rafi Fernandez, Christine France,
Silvano Franco, Shirley Gill, Deh-Ta Hsiung,
Christine Ingram, Peter Jordan, Norma MacMillan,
Maggie Mayhew, Annie Nicholls, Maggie Pannell, Katherine
Richmond, Anne Sheasby, Liz Trigg,
Steven Wheeler, Jeni Wright

Photography: William Adams-Lingwood, Karl Adamson,
Edward Allwright, John Freeman, Amanda Heywood,
Janine Hosegood, David Jordan, Don Last,
Patrick McLeavey, Michael Michaels, Thomas Odulate

A CIP catalogue record for this book is available from the
British Library

COOK'S NOTES

Bracketed terms are intended for American readers.

For all recipes, quantities are given in both metric and imperial
measures and, where appropriate, in standard cups and spoons.
Follow one set of measures, but not a mixture, because they are
not interchangeable.

Standard spoon and cup measures are level. 1 tsp = 5ml, 1 tbsp =
15ml, 1 cup = 250ml/8fl oz. Australian standard tablespoons are
20ml. Australian readers should use 3 tsp
in place of 1 tbsp for measuring small quantities.

American pints are 16fl oz/2 cups. American readers should use
20fl oz/2.5 cups in place of 1 pint when measuring liquids.

Electric oven temperatures in this book are for conventional
ovens. When using a fan oven, the temperature will probably
need to be reduced by about 10–20°C/20–40°F. Since ovens
vary, you should check with your manufacturer's instruction
book for guidance.

Medium (US large) eggs are used unless otherwise stated.

PUBLISHER'S NOTE:
Although the advice and information in this book are believed
to be accurate and true at the time of going to press, neither the
authors nor the publisher can accept any legal responsibility or
liability for any errors or omissions that may have been made nor
for any inaccuracies nor for any loss, harm or injury that comes
about from following instructions or advice in this book.